Shahnawaz Alam

# Using Security Patterns in Web -Application

Anchor Academic
Publishing

**Alam, Shahnawaz: Using Security Patterns in Web -Application. Hamburg, Anchor Academic Publishing 2014**

Buch-ISBN: 978-3-95489-266-2
PDF-eBook-ISBN: 978-3-95489-766-7
Druck/Herstellung: Anchor Academic Publishing, Hamburg, 2014

**Bibliografische Information der Deutschen Nationalbibliothek:**
Die Deutsche Nationalbibliothek verzeichnet diese Publikation in der Deutschen Nationalbibliografie; detaillierte bibliografische Daten sind im Internet über http://dnb.d-nb.de abrufbar.

**Bibliographical Information of the German National Library:**
The German National Library lists this publication in the German National Bibliography. Detailed bibliographic data can be found at: http://dnb.d-nb.de


Hermannstal 119k, 22119 Hamburg
http://www.diplomica-verlag.de, Hamburg 2014
Printed in Germany

## Acknowledgements

I would like to take this opportunity to thank the following persons for their input, help and support:

- Dr Chez Ciechanowic for his support throughout this paper
- I would like to express my appreciation to all the professors at Royal Holloway who have increased my understanding of Information Security, without which this paper would not have been possible.
- Last, but not least, my parents and family for their kindness, support and encouragement.

## Abstract

Web-Application have been widely accepted by the organization be it in private, public or government sector and form the main part of any e-commerce business on the internet.

However with the widespread of web-application, the threats related to the web-application have also emerged. Web-application transmit substantial amount of critical data such as password or credit card information etc and this data should be protected from an attacker.

There has been huge number of attacks on the web-application such as 'SQL Injection', 'Cross-Site Scripting', 'Http Response Splitting' in recent years and it is one of the main concerns in both the software developer and security professional community.

This projects aims to explore how security can be incorporated by using security pattern in web-application and how effective it is in addressing the security problems of web-application.

## Table of Contents

## List of figures

# Chapter 1: Introduction

## 1.1 Problems

In these advance world where paper had changed its form to electronic version and office had moved itself to cloud making the entire world very small place to communicate. People have become more inclined towards the technology due to the advances in technologies as their work can be done conveniently and faster than the normal scenario.

The advances in the technologies and the widespread of internet had come up with lots of advantages and disadvantages. On one hand internet had made the task very simple for a human being and one great examples is the discovery of email for sending letter to your friend, relatives etc is just a matter of seconds to anywhere in the world, as compared to olden days where if you want to send letter to someone living in abroad you have to wait fifteen days for the letter to be delivered. There are many such examples about the advantages these technologies had brought to us and the list is never ending.

On the other hand due to the widespread of internet and the huge acceptance of technologies in business community had developed a series of problem in the world. Also with the introduction of e-commerce in business further worsen the issues as business houses started doing business on the internet through readymade web-application developed by big brand such as Microsoft or Java Software or in-house web-application development.

These web-applications and business software's had become one of the major targets for attacker because of the fact that many critical information can be derived such as credit card information, login credentials etc, from such attack and which can later be used for some financials benefits. Attack such as eavesdropping, exploiting poor authentication system, tampering the system log, cross-site scripting, SQL injection attack and HTTP Response Splitting are some of the most common attacks and very large in numbers.

One of the main reasons behind all this attack and which are already been proved by the industry experts and researcher is poor coding and design flaws of the web-application or software system. The developer who does the development of the web-application usually is not aware of the security and their main point of concentration is the functionality part of the application rather than its security implications.

Therefore, a solution should come up which will bridge up this gap between the development and security community. Additionally, the solution should also serves as the remedies for the attack which are identified above and helps in developing secure software and web-application.

In my thesis I have spoken about this solution in more detail so that the subject can easily be understood.

## 1.2 Aim and Objectives

**Aim:** The aim of this paper is to explore how security is incorporated by using security pattern in web-application.

**Objectives:** The Preliminary objective of this dissertation is as follows:

a. Introduce web-application and web-application security

b. Introduce design pattern and Security Pattern

The Main objective is to:

a. Identify a set of security patterns which can be used to address the issues in web-application

b. How effective these security patterns are in addressing the problems?

c. What are the benefits and liabilities of implementing this pattern in web-application?

d. Justify that security pattern actually improves the security of the web-application with proper example.

## 1.3 Structure:

The structure of paper is divided in four phase where each phase also includes chapters.

**Phase 1** – This phase consists of two chapters where it provides introduction to web-application and web-application security along with attack and countermeasures to attack.

**Phase 2** – This phase consists of two chapters where it provides introduction to design pattern and security pattern.

**Phase 3** - This phase consists of two chapters where the security patterns are identified and also the implementation of the security pattern had been discussed in details along with their benefits and liabilities after implementation. This phase consist all of the work

**Phase 4**- This phase consist of conclusion drawn from this thesis.

# Chapter 2: Background on Web Application & Web Application Security

## 2.1 Background of Web- Application

Over the past 20 years, web had benefitted millions of businesses and served as the channel for the customer to communicate with the businesses for exchanging information. According to the survey more than 1 billion user uses internet today [Source - Computer Industry Almanac, 2006] and in the U.S alone the U.S e-commerce spending accounted for $102.1 billion in 2006[Source-comScore Networks, 2007]

Before explaining Web Application I would like to say the fundamental part of web application which is the word "application". As said by Bob Baxley the word application means "a computer program designed for a specific task or use" [1]

In his document he also said that "The Fundamental purpose of all web applications is to facilitate the completion of one or more tasks" [2].

To start with the conversation I will categorize website into two forms: [3]

a. Content - Based Website.
b. Website Based for Service.

Content based website is the website which we can see in day to day life such as BBC News, ISBN Sports, Times of India etc. This kind of website is basically used for information where you can visit and read necessary information whereas the later which is service-oriented website are used for some specific task to be performed by the visitor of the website.Users who visit this kind of site have some objective to visit the website. This service –oriented based website is support by the application servers and a database servers in background which used web browser to interact with end user or client and is also known as web-application. One of the best examples of web-application is email where company like Google and Rediffmail is providing the web-based mailing client.

The most significant benefit of web-application that its need a web-browser as a client to interact with back end server. Web application follows the architecture of client-server environment. Client –Server environment can be explained as an environment where multiple computers have access and share the information such as entering private date into the database. [4]

The designer who develop the web-application does not have to worry to develop the client end for accessing the application for a specific computer or operating system as it uses the web browser as client that can run on any platform be it Mac, Windows or Linux. However some of the web-application only supports browser like Windows Explorer and Firefox and they are browser specific.

The technology commonly used in developing the web –application is the combination of server –side scripting such as ASP, PHP, JSP and client- side scripting known as HTML, DHTML, and JavaScript etc. The client –side deals with the overall presentation of the website and server-side takes care of the more vital part of the web-application such as storing or retrieving data from the database.

Another significant benefit of the web-application is that it can easily be implemented without much installation requirement and can also be easily deployed anywhere at no cost.

One of the vital aspects of web –application is how this web-application works? To explain the understanding of web –application operation, I will take a support of the Figure 1.1 to illustrate the operation of web –application:

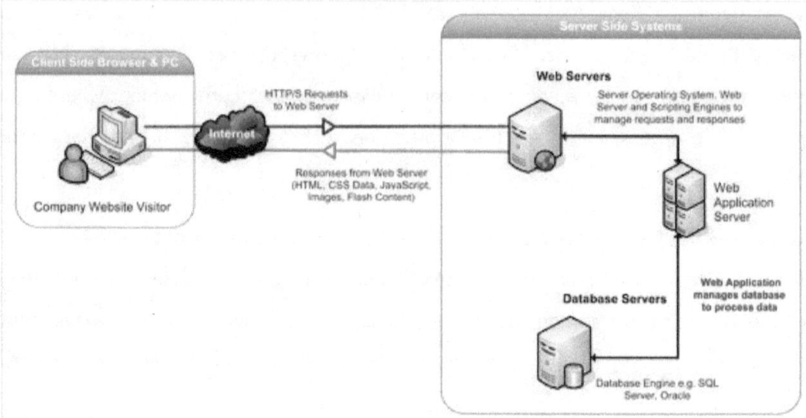


**Figure 1 the operation of Web Application [5]**

In the Figure above shows that the visitor had visit the company website and the initial request had been triggered by the visitor via browser to the web-server which is then forwarded to the web-application. The web-application in response to the request had accessed the database and performs the task requested such as modifying or retrieving the content of the database. After the process had been completed, the web-application then represents the information to the user via browser.

However, the future of web-application is going towards a new generation of web-application where the web-application will not need any backend server to store or retrieve data. It will be similar to the way you save your word document on your computer and it does not need server to the save that document on to the desktop.

## 2.2 Background on Web Application Security

The vulnerabilities in software had increased at an unexpected rate and in the year 2006, National Institute of Standards and Technology [NIST] National Vulnerability Database had recorded the informed vulnerability to something over 6,600 vulnerabilities. Due to these vulnerabilities a new trend had been emerged and the software community started including the security in their design and development phase which has resulted into overall improvement to operating system security.

As the operating system had become more secure there had been a shift in the hacker community. They started targeting the application layer vulnerabilities instead of operating system vulnerabilities. [6]

The changing business environment together with the advances in web-technologies has leaded the organization to adopt the web-application by default. Today any organization whether is it public, private or government sector depends solely on web-application to interact with customer or client.

Although the adoption of web-application in business community gives greater efficiency and convenience, it's give rise to the new threat in security, which can be of significant risk to an organization if the I.T. Infrastructure of the organization had not been handled carefully.

As the web-application can be easily deployed, its growth is beyond expectation and due to this trend in web-application, I.T. Infrastructure became more complex and distributed which are harder to maintain from the security perspective. From almost a decade if you see then most of the organization had been dependent on the firewall for their security in order to protect their I.T Infrastructure. However now trends had been changed, hacker community is no longer targeting network perimeter such as firewall to gain access to the organization resources instead they are targeting more on the security flaws of the web-application design such as injection flaws, improper input validation etc. Therefore deploying of network perimeter will not be enough for the safeguard of web-application, a more robust security implementation is required to safeguard application from such threats.

The threats are generated in different way such as dishonest user, session-less protocols, insecure network and complex web technologies. In web-application the client end are not basically controlled by the owner of the application. Hence the input by a client cannot be fully trusted and processed directly. An attacker can masquerade as a legitimate user and thus create false message and cookies. In addition to this, HTTP is a session-less protocol and it is subjected to attack such as replay and injection attack.The HTTP Message can be easily tampered which will result in modified message and due widespread of spoofing software it can easily be spoofed or sniffed. [7]

According to the "2002 Computer Crime and Security Survey" conducted by Computer Security Institute & San Francisco FBI Computer Intrusion Squad.

"Web application incidents cost companies more than $320,000,000 in 2001."

44% respondent to the 2002 Computer Crime and Security Survey were willing and able to quantify their financial losses .These respondents reported $455,848,000 in financial losses. [8]

Therefore the organization should understand the risk and threats properly in order to implement appropriate countermeasures or safeguard. Additionally both the technical and administrative security control must be reinforced for the security of the critical I.T. Infrastructure in response to the web-application deployment.

# Chapter 3: Attacks and Countermeasures of Web - Application

With the increase in adoptability of the web-application by different organization comprises of private, public and government sector had given birth to different kind of attack on web-application.

The Open Web Application Security Project had become the industry de-facto guidelines for developing secure web-application software. The OWASP is free accessible worldwide and serves as the standard for secure development, However it is not regarded as standard officially and it's just states a set of guidelines which are to be followed during web-application development.

The OWASP had listed the top ten vulnerabilities such as Cross-Site Scripting, Injection Flaws, and Malicious File Extension etc. The total list of the TOP TEN vulnerabilities of web application can be found on www.owasp.org

In this section of the project I will be discussing some of the most fundamental attack from the developer perspective in regard to web-application such as Eavesdropping, Poor Authentication Mechanism, Log Tempering, SQL Injection and Cross-Site Scripting and its countermeasures. However If the developer develop code by keeping in mind the security implication of the web-application then this kind of attack can be avoided. The details are discussed later on this thesis.

## 3.1 Eavesdropping

### 3.1.1 What is Eavesdropping?

Intercepting real-time private communication traffic in an unauthorized way is known as Eavesdropping. Some of the examples are insecure data transmission between computers, VOIP calls etc. The term eavesdrop had been derived from the word eaves which mean standing under the eaves of the house and listening the private conversation without the knowledge of the other. [9]

### 3.1.2 How Eavesdropping happen?

In my example of explanation I will be taking the scenario of the normal LAN network where all computers into the network are using the common shared media such as HUB to communicate with each other. Eavesdropping attack can be implemented in this kind of network.

In a normal network, the network interface card is usually set to a non-promiscuous mode by default and the network card is only bothered about the traffic intended to his address and leaves the other traffic. Eavesdropping attack is conducted by an attacker by setting the network interface card to promiscuous mode. Once this mode is activated the network interface card capture all traffic irrespective of its destination address ,thus an attacker can read all the traffic and can derived the password or other valuable information from the traffic if the traffic is not encrypted or secure.[10]

There are several tools available in the marketplace for eavesdropping such as 'tcpdump' [11] and ethereal [12].

### 3.1.3 Countermeasures for Eavesdropping

In this section I would be explaining the countermeasures from the perspective of web-application. As stated above that the attack happen on the network layer then how its effect the working of web-application. Following the attack, suppose an user entered his credit card detail in an website which has to processed for his payment online and during the transmission of this data, an attacker had intercepted it ,thus an attacker has a credit card information of the customer which he can used it later.

Therefore the most effective countermeasures suggested for this attack are as follows:

Proper segmentation of the network should be done and a strong security physical security should be placed. We have to first locally secure the traffic such as inside organization building or office.

The traffic should be fully encrypted during the transmission from one node to another node or one LAN to another LAN.A proper implementation of SSL and IPSEC should be done in order to provide a secure communication between nodes. [13]

## 3.2 Exploiting Poor Authentication

### 3.2.1 What is Poor Authentication?

In my example of explaining poor authentication I will take the most conventional authentication method of username and password which is widely used across every domain. Also most of the web-application used this conventional method to authenticate the client. One of the most significant weaknesses of this authentication method is that client usually uses weak password which are easy to guess and also sometime this client uses the same password across other domain for authentication.

Therefore an attacker can easily derive the password and used it for unauthorized access to the client resources.

### 3.2.2 How the poor authentication can be exploited?

As stated above that the client usually choose easy password which can be easily guessed. Following this scenario an attacker would deploy a dictionary attack which contain the list of most commonly used password. The dictionary attack will try the entire commonly used password on to the system for access till it successfully logged in and thus an attacker have a password which he can use and masquerade as a legitimate client to web-application and perform the task which he is not authorized to do.

### 3.2.3 Countermeasures of poor authentication

Several countermeasures had been suggested in the literature but among them the most common countermeasures are as follows:

a. User should choose strong password with a combination of digits, special characters, mixing of capital and small alphabets etc.
b. User should follow the principle of One-Time Password where the password should be used only once to login to the system.
c. Strong security policy should be implemented by the administrator of the web-application for choosing password.
d. Dual –authentication system should be implemented to the web-application for better and reliable authentication process.

## 3.3 Log Tampering

### 3.3.1 Overview of Log

In the most common language log can be explained as the data which are maintain by the system and it contains event log of the operating system component. This log files contain information such as changes in devices, driver, system, event etc. [14]

### 3.3.2 What is log tampering?

These attacks basically target the log file on the system. An attacker first tries to access the log files of system and then injects, modify or forge log entries into the log file of the system. As an attacker had modified the log entries, this modified log easily mislead a log audit, hence the attacker is successful in covering the traces of attack and can easily perform the unauthorized actions on to the system. To deploy this attack, an attacker firstly observes the system and he can have some knowledge about the logging format of the system as well. The attacker after his homework starts attacking the system either directly by modifying the content of the log files or through a log injection who are specially implemented into the system which will write logs.

### 3.3.3 Countermeasures for Log Tampering

Some of the common countermeasures for mitigating the log tampering are as follows:

a. Control the access of the log files carefully.
b. A proper input validation mechanism should be placed so that any tainted data are not allowed to be written in to the log files without proper data validation.
c. To control the flow of execution, a proper synchronization mechanism should be placed.
d. Tools should be used to identify the log forging vulnerabilities. [15]

## 3.4 SQL Injection

### 3.4.1 Overview of SQL injection

SQL Injection which is also commonly known as injection flaws and they are very common in most of the web application.

These attacks happen when the user supplies a set of data which are sent to the interpreter for a command or query. The attacker tricks the interpreter by sending the specially crafted data in order to execute the unintended commands. If the attack is successful then the attacker has access to application and he can create, read, modify and delete any data. In the worst case scenario an attacker will have the entire control of the application and the underlying system. [16]

### 3.4.2 Countermeasures for SQL Injection

The entire things happen due to the implementation of interpreter into the web-application. Therefore the use of interpreter into the application should be avoided and including of using the save API should be highly adopted.

## 3.5 Cross-Site Scripting

### 3.5.1 What is Cross-Site Scripting?

Cross-Site scripting which is also known as XSS is one of the most common attacks which an attacker uses to hack web-application today. The main objective of the cross-site scripting is to attack the privacy of the user of a particular website and if they are successful in fulfilling their objective then the entire security of the website is collapsed.

Usually in most of the attack, the attack metric consist of an attacker and website or the other way round an attacker and the user client but in this attack its consists of all the three components an attacker, user and website. The main objective of the CSS attack is to steal the cookies of the user so that an attacker can use those cookies to masquerade as a legitimate user to website. The attacker runs a malicious JavaScript on the user's browser with access rights of the website. These malicious JavaScript help the attacker to retrieve the cookies and masquerade as a legitimate user. [17]

### 3.5.2 Countermeasure of Cross-Site Scripting

To protect the website from cross-site scripting attacks, some of the most important countermeasures are-

a. A best practice of input filtering should be applied. This is also known as input sanitation. This filter should do advance filtering of HTML tag and also include JavaScript code in its filtering.
b. A well versed out-filtering should be deployed so it can put on check on the data which is sent back to the browser rather than when it is received by the script.
c. By deploying the application level firewall which can detect the CSS attack and malicious script and block it on the gateway itself.

## 3.6 HTTP Response Splitting

### 3.6.1 What is HTTP Response Splitting?

HTTP Response splitting is the new type of attack in the world of web-application. These attacks also help in mounting other attack such as Cross-Site Scripting Attack, Web Cache Attack etc.

In this attack, three entities are involved which are as follows:

a. Web Server: - Server where the web-site is hosted.
b. Target: Basically some kind of proxy or cache server which talk to web-server on behalf of the attacker. A cache web browser can also be used as the target.
c. Attacker: The person who attack the system.

The attacker deploy this attack by sending a HTTP request to the web server in such a way that its forces the server to generated output stream which is then interpreted by the target system as two http response instead of one. Once the attacker is successful in splitting the HTTP response in two responses, the attacker sends the two requests through the target where the first request generates two responses from the web server and other request would be some resource on the web server.

However in regard to the second request, it will be matched with the second http response by the web server. This second request is entirely controlled by the attacker and attacker will tactfully make the target believe that the resource of the web-server is the server HTTP Response. With this attack, an attacker can mount different attack which I have already stated above. [18]

### 3.6.2 Countermeasure for HTTP Response Splitting

Some of the most important countermeasure for HTTP Response splitting is as follows:

a. A proper input validation mechanism should be place in web-application. So that it verify input parameter at both side client side as well as server side.
b. Output Sanitation is another important mechanism which should be placed because redisplaying or echoing the data possess a significant risk to the web –application.
c. Secure Transport should be done, if the communication between the client and server is secured than the chance of replaying the data will be less. This can be done by implementing SSL, IPsec etc. [19]

## 3.7 Reason of Attack on Web Application

One of the most significant reasons behind all this attack is the weakness in the development of web-application. The security implication had not been taken care during the design and development phase of the application which leads to design flaws and vulnerabilities which were further exploited by the attacker to attack the system.

As you in development community most emphasis had been given to design and functionality of the product and to make their design flawless, the developer community had come up with a concept known as "Design Pattern" which is derived from a main concept of Alexander Christopher. This concept had been wide accepted through the development community. Companies like Microsoft and sun microsystem started adopting this concept for their development cycle.

Similarly, to fulfill the gap between the functionality and security implication of the product, a new concept had been derived known as "Security Patterns". This concept had been widely accepted in the developer community as the developer can develop software irrespective whether he has knowledge about security or not. Thus the gap between the developer and security community had been addressed by the discovery of security pattern.

Both the concept of "Design Pattern" and "Security Pattern" had been discussed in detail in chapter 4 and chapter 5.

# Chapter 4: Introduction to Patterns

## 4.1. An introduction to pattern language

Before I start my explanation about security pattern which I have mention on the above chapter, I would like to bring your notice on the root of the security pattern and how this root had helped in deriving the idea of developing security pattern for the information security field.

At late 1960s Christopher Alexander who is a brick and mortar architect, together with his team had indulged themselves in the development of a new method of planning and architecture and started analyzing how people interact with the physical spaces. [20] After several years of experiment they had published number of book where they had mentioned that human life is of full patterns which a human follows on to their day to day life. In his book he also mentioned that if you see the entire human life then it is a kind of architecture and this architecture basically supports these patterns which make a human life better and complacent.

Therefore according the Christopher he says "A pattern language is really nothing more than a precise way of describing someone's experience of a building" [21]

Alexander observation has a format which is most commonly known as "Design Pattern" where it contains the summary of the context of problems and its related solutions.

The group of any related design pattern is commonly known as "Design Language"

Later, these concepts of pattern language had been adopted by the computer science field not through user interface designer but through initiative of programming community. The method of documenting the problems along with solutions so that it serves as the guidelines in addressing repeating problem of the programming have been widely adopted in programming community. Additionally, the idea behind associating this pattern into hierarchical structure of the pattern language had developed parallels for design in object-oriented software. [22]

According to James Coplien of Bell Laboratories comments "Focusing on objects had caused us to lose the system perspective. Preoccupation with design method had caused us to lose the human perspective. The curious parallels between Alexander's

World of buildings and our world of software construction helped the ideas to take root and thrive in grassroots programming communities worldwide. The Pattern discipline has become one of the most widely applied and important ideas of the past decade in software architecture and design."[23]

Of late the software community started a series of research and conferences on the pattern languages of programming for new development and use of design pattern in software design. This revolution in the software community is the place where the "Design Pattern" had been first created.

## 4.2. What is Design Pattern?

Different people have different understanding and definition about the design pattern but I would go according to the software community.

According to the software industry the definition of the term design pattern is

"A Design pattern is essentially a description of a commonly occurring object-oriented design problem and how to solve it" [24]

Design pattern consist a technique of capturing existing software design so that it can be reuse effectively. [25]

Design pattern basically explain the idea where a collaborating object and classes are customized for addressing the specific design problem. This pattern is in the form catalogue where the informal description of their function is provided. However, how effectively it will be used in design environment is left totally on the organization and the experience of the programmer. [26]

Later an effective approach had been taken for making this pattern used in a systematic manner during software design phase. This approach is known as Pattern Oriented Technique. Most of the methodologies and approach used in the software community, usually groups a set of classes as class categories or subsystems and these class categories or subsystem are not treated as reusable units. They are used only as a mechanism for managing the structural complexity. In contrast POT serves the building blocks of an object oriented design. [27]

Unlike many design methodologies which provide only one solution to the specific design problem, design pattern offer range of solution to the developer in context to the design problem.

Hence design pattern had become very popular and are widely adopted by the software community as a guidelines for solving the design problem. Developer and programmer follow this design pattern as their benchmark while developing and programming the software or application.

## 4.3 History of Design Pattern

The history of design pattern is as follows:

a. In the year 1970s, Christopher Alexander, a brick and mortar architect, had proposed visually pleasing and practical structures for a certain application and setting which could be described by a pattern language.
b. In 1987, Kent Beck and Ward Cunningham presented an OOPSLA paper titled Using pattern languages for Object-Oriented Programs.
c. In the late 1980s and early 1990s a number of individuals began to look at the problem of identifying and describing patterns used to create software.
d. In 1995, the now-classic text Design Patterns by Erich Gamma, Richard Helm, Ralph Johnson, and John Vlissides was published. The authors are often called the Gang of Four [GOF].In his books he described Design patterns is essentially a catalogue of 23 commonly occurring problems in object-oriented design and a pattern solve each one. [28]

## 4.4 Design Pattern Template

The design pattern templates had been originally taken from original Alexander Christopher templates.

The design template is as follows:

a. **Name:** Name of the Pattern
b. **Type:** Pattern type such as whether it is design or organizational or structural pattern.
c. **Problem:** What is the problem the pattern needs to be solved which should be put in detail and simple?
d. **Context:** The context of the problem
e. **Forces:** The motivation or issues in solving the problems
f. **Solutions:** The solutions for the above stated problem should be put in detail.
g. **Consequences:** The result of implementing the solution both the benefit and liabilities side of the solution should be documented and stated.
h. **Relate Patterns:** Related pattern which address the same problem.

# Chapter 5: An Introduction to Security Patterns

## 5.1 What is Security Pattern?

Before I explain about security pattern I would like to say what the term "Pattern" actually means is "A pattern is a formalization of a problem/ solution pair which are used to make decision" [29]

Different literature on security pattern had described it in a different way but I will go with the most generic definition of security pattern.

Definition: "A Security Pattern describes a particular recurring security problem that arises in a specific context and presents a well-proven generic scheme for its solution." [30]

In recent years the number of security attack had been increased unexpectedly and security had become one of the essential components in the software development community. Researcher had proven that design error and code error is one of the major cause of vulnerabilities in to the software which are later explored by an attacker to attack the system.

Therefore, in order to develop the secure software, secure software architecture and design had become essential requirement by the software industry. Of late security of software had become one of the most important factors in the evaluation of software quality. The entire shift towards the security aspect in software development had lead to the development of the concept known as "Security Pattern".

Security Pattern basically document best practice to solve the problems in security which are arising frequently in the software development community and also encourage others in reusing the proven expert solution in context to the problem. [31]

To clarify your understanding of what is security pattern in a more precise way I will take an example to explain in brief.

Suppose a developer had been given a task of developing the application features which are to be implemented, Let`s say for example that an developer had been asked to develop a simple user login features into the application. These login modules contain simple flow of execution that it's collect username and password from the user and then compare it with database to authenticate the user to the application. Thus when the developer start developing this module, he will simply concentrate on the functional aspect of the module and how the module should work till the end result.

He will not consider the security aspect of the module as it is not his work and because of this he will simply ignore the security best practice in both his approach of designing and coding the module.

This is where security pattern play a very vital role. Consider a situation where the developer has a pre-existing security design which can be used by a developer for implementing the features. A design that takes care of the possible attack on his module and which also contains the security best-practice in regard to his module.

Now, the developer does not have to worry about How, why and where the security features has to be implemented. [32]

"A security pattern can be regarded as the recipe for solving the security problems in software and web application development community"

## 5.2 History of Security Pattern

Some of the major developments in Security Pattern field in recent years are as follows:

a. In 1997, Yoder and Barcalow were the first who published the paper related to Security Pattern. In their paper they have identified seven important security pattern known as singles access point pattern, checkpoint pattern, roles pattern, session pattern, full view with errors pattern, limited view pattern, secure access layer pattern.
b. Braga et al. presented a pattern on cryptography known as Tropyc .Its consists of nine pattern related to the field of cryptography for developing software with cryptographic

components. The main idea of this pattern is to bring traditional aspect of security such as confidentiality, integrity, authentication and non-repudiation into software or application design.

c. Later Brown et al, also presented a pattern known as Authenticator pattern which basically take care of the access request done by user to the resource and perform decision based on the access policy defined.
d. Fernandez, presented pattern known as Access Control Pattern and also pattern such as authorization rules and role-based access control pattern. This set of pattern deals with the security issues related to access control in software or application development.
e. Furthermore, the work is going on the different architectural level pattern which has different level of security requirement at different architectural level. [33]

## 5.3 Why Security Pattern?

This is one the most important question as why do we really need security pattern?

If you see in broader perspective then in a real world scenario you will see that there is huge disconnect between the developer and the security professional. Developer are more concerned about the functional aspect of the application and they really don`t care about how security should be integrated into the application design and coding. However security professional are more inclined towards the security issue in the application design and development. This gap between the developer and security professional should be filled for the secure software or application development.

To fill this huge gap between the developer and security professional, an idea of security pattern had been discovered.

As I have already explained how security pattern adds value into the field of software or application security with the help of an example I would like to conclude that Security pattern can be regarded as "Foundation for developing secure software" and are of great importance to the field of Information Security as the development of secure software will lead to a overall development in the security and thus address the basic aspect of information security i.e. confidentiality, integrity, availability and non-repudiation.

## 5.4 Types of Security Pattern

There are only two types of security pattern which are as follows:

**Structural Patterns:** The patterns which are implemented into the final products are known as Structural Pattern. This pattern follows the idea of design pattern such as those which is used by the Gang of Four. The patterns often consist of diagram of structure and its descriptions of interactions.

**Procedural Patterns:** These patterns are used as an improvement to the process of developing security-critical software. Since it acts as an improvement to the development process it often have impact over the management or organization of a development project. [34]

## 5.5 Use and Misuse Case in Security Pattern.

In Security pattern we a have terminology called use and misuse case. I would be describing both the terminology in detail:

**Use Case in Security Pattern:**

Use Case in Security pattern is the scenario where the pattern is used such as authentication pattern in a web-application. Suppose a user visited to the bank website, enters his login credential and after the user had been authenticated by the web-application, user check its balance and then logged off. This use case does not taken into consideration the attack metric of the login procedure. This a simple implementation of security pattern where it does not think from the perspective of an attacker.

**Misuse Case in Security Pattern:**

Misuse case sometime also known as misuse pattern. This misuse case describe from the perspective of an attacker, how an attacker can perform an attack by taking the advantage of vulnerabilities of some environment. This misuse case basically helps the developer to think from the attacker point of view and counteract its development process as well as helps in gathering information which is needed at each stage of the attack. In a broader sense, a misuse case basically emphasize on the unauthorized use of the information and the attack step on a particular system or web application. [35]

## 5.6 Security Pattern Template

Different people use different security pattern template according to their convenience but I would be discussing the default security pattern which had been derived from the design pattern template.

a. **Pattern Name:** The name of the security pattern which should be in concise manner.
b. **Pattern Abstract:** The abstract of the patterns consist the summary about what is the purpose of the pattern.
c. **Aliases:** The other name of the pattern, such as the name by which it has been addressed in other literature.
d. **Problem:** This section of the pattern template explains the condition in which the pattern can be used. It also explains the motivation behind using the pattern.
e. **Solution:** This section explains how the problem had been solved by the pattern which had been described on the problem statement. It also explains how it is applicable to the problem and what the rationale behind applying the solutions.
f. **Static Structure:** It basically represent the important elements which are involved when the pattern are used.
g. **Dynamic Structure:** These represent the interactions between the important elements in the static structure.
h. **Implementation Issues:** This section includes issues which could arise when the pattern are used during the implementation phase. The most significant issue should be address first and the least significant could be taken care later.

i. **Common Attacks:** It should indentify the common attacks which can happen with this pattern. The section basically enlightens you with scenario where the properly implemented pattern can also be attack.

j. **Known Uses:** This is where you can include example of the actual use of the pattern in the real world.

k. **Sample Code:** As the developer are fond of source code because they can link their coding into their application and can start using the code immediately. Though the pattern does not really is the source of source code but it is usually good if some kind of sample code can be presented for better understanding of the developer.

l. **Consequences:** These sections explain the benefits and liabilities of applying the pattern with respect to different software or web-application development.

m. **Related Pattern:** These sections include the list of other related problem which addresses the same problems which are given in the problem statement.

n. **References:** This section consists of reference in regard to the pattern in different literature and on web. [36]

# Chapter 6: Overview and Implementation of Security Patterns

This phase of my project is one of the most important parts in my thesis. Before I start I would like to enlighten you about the methodologies I have used in this section to explain my concept. In this section I will be discussing security pattern which can be used for addressing the attack which are explained above. I will start with the overview of the security pattern which I have identified and used for resolving the issues and then I will discuss the implementation aspect of the security pattern and its related pattern in detail and how this implementation is basically addressing the attack in a form of a summary.

I will end with researcher view about the security pattern with help of an example and what I feel about security pattern as a whole.

Also during my demonstration of security pattern implementation I will not use security pattern template instead I will used simple flow of language so that the thing can be easily understood.

I would also include the implementation source code to support your understand of security pattern and it will be presented in Appendices section of this thesis

## 6.1 Overview of Security Pattern used to address attack

### 6.1.1 Secure Pipe Pattern

These patterns play a very vital role in establishing the secure communication between the client and the servers or vice versa when trading happen online between the trading partners or between the customer and the company.

In a distributed network web application where there will be combination of different requirement in regard to security related to client, servers or any other intermediaries. Therefore standardizing this security requirement between internal and external parties using the same platform and security mechanism will not be easy task.

In such an environment these patterns add value by providing mutual authentication between parties and which in turn established services such as confidentiality and non-repudiation.

This service is essentially critical from the point of business to business integration using web services.

This secure pipe pattern is used in the technologies such as HTTPS, SSL/TLS, IPSEC etc. The related security pattern for this pattern is Message Interceptor Gateway.

### 6.1.2 Secure Proxy Pattern

Secure proxy pattern are used to secure and control access of distributed application components which are exposed as the web facing services. It acts as a secure proxy to provide common interface to the underlying distributed application components and restrict its direct access. The Secure Proxy pattern can be implemented for basic level authentication.[40] The technologies or standard who had implemented this pattern are Servlets, JAX –RPC and SAAJ. The related pattern for secure proxy pattern is Intercepting Web Agent, Secure Message router, Message Interceptor Gateway and Extract Adapter. [37]

### 6.1.3 Secure Logger Pattern

This pattern helps the application in defining the way of how an application can capture the event and exceptions in a secure and reliable way so that it cannot be modified by an attacker. This pattern makes sure that the log is secure and can be easily used for security audit in future. The secure logger pattern had been implemented by JMX, Java API for logging and the related pattern of secure logger pattern is secure pipe pattern.However the secure pipe pattern does not do any function related to logging the event but in contrast it serves one of the vital functions for securely logging the system log into secure log store which will be discussed later.

### 6.1.4 Intercepting Validator Pattern

This pattern is one of the most important patterns used in the web-application development as this pattern serves the purpose of validating the input by client to the web-application.

Unchecked input can lead to the number of problem in a web-application such as buffer overflow, SQL injection etc.

These data validations consist of validation on data types, data format, data length, data range and null – value handling. [41] The technologies which had implemented this pattern are JSP and Servlets and the related pattern for this pattern are Message Inspector and Message Inspector Gateway. [38]

## 6.2 Implementation of Security Pattern in Context to Attack

### 6.2.1 Mitigating Eavesdropping with Secure Pipe and its Related Pattern

As stated above that eavesdropping happen because of the insecure communication channel and a mechanism should be put into place to prevent the privacy of the communication which can be tampered by eavesdropping and man-in-the middle attack.

From the perspective of an web-application ,all client transaction should be protected because this transaction are often exposed to different kind of attack such as eavesdropping, spoofing and replay attacks. Whenever a request transmits through an insecure network, this request are intercepted and exposed by an attacker. To avoid this organization started using VPN but even in VPN, data are exposed to endpoints such as inside an organization or more precisely inside intranets. Once the data are exposed it can be modified, disclosed or duplicated.

Also the use of network sniffer to capture the data leads to the problem where even a very new attacker can get hold of the unencrypted credentials and credit card information.

This entire problem occurs because of the fact that the business application does business over an insecure and untrusted network known as internet. The content-based website are not the primary target of the attacker but the web-application which transmit sensitive information such as credit card information is usually the main target of an attacker as he can used that information in future for financial benefits.

The constraint in addressing this problem of insecure communication is that the developer should avoid writing application logic for providing protection. Instead it is better to integrate the solution to the infrastructure level so that complexity into application can be avoided. Secondly a hardware device should be placed in order to speed up cryptographic algorithms which are needed to prevent confidentiality and integrity issues. Thirdly proven third party products have to be adopted for providing reliable data and communication security and lastly one have to limit the processing of all data as its result in bad performance and delay in encryption.

The solution to the entire problem and constraint in solving the problem is the implementation of Secure Pipe Pattern.

Secure Pipe basically guarantees the integrity and data privacy which transmits over an insecure network.

A secure pipe gives a simple and standardized way to secure the data over an insecure network. Also secure pipe does not require application layer logic which reduces its complexity in implementation. In some case the implementation of secure pipe are even moved off from both the application and hardware level altogether. However since the secure pipe relies on the encryption and decryption of the entire data which are sent over it, it possess some kind of performance issues. Secure pipe gives options to developer of delegating the processing to the hardware accelerators which are indented to do that task only.

I will explain the working of the secure pipe pattern with the aid of a diagram which is as follows:

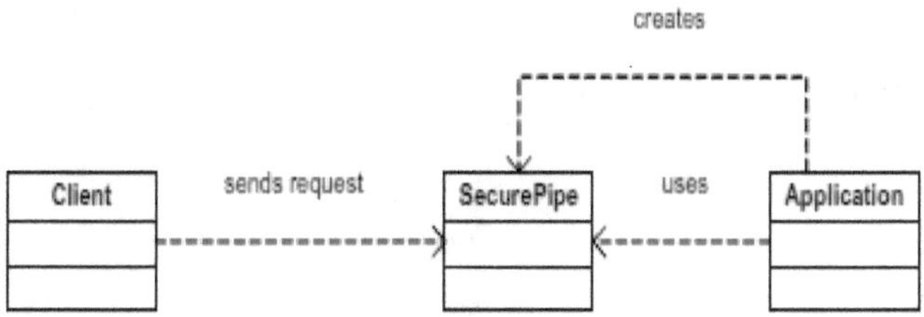


**Figure 2: Secure Pipe Pattern Diagram [39]**

In the above figure Client first initiates a login with the application, once the application receives the client initiation the applications creates a system level secure pipe on which the secure communication will take place between the client and application. This secure pipe provides a secure communication channel to provide privacy and integrity of data between client and application.

The sequence diagram will explain how the entire mechanism of secure pipe pattern works in detail.

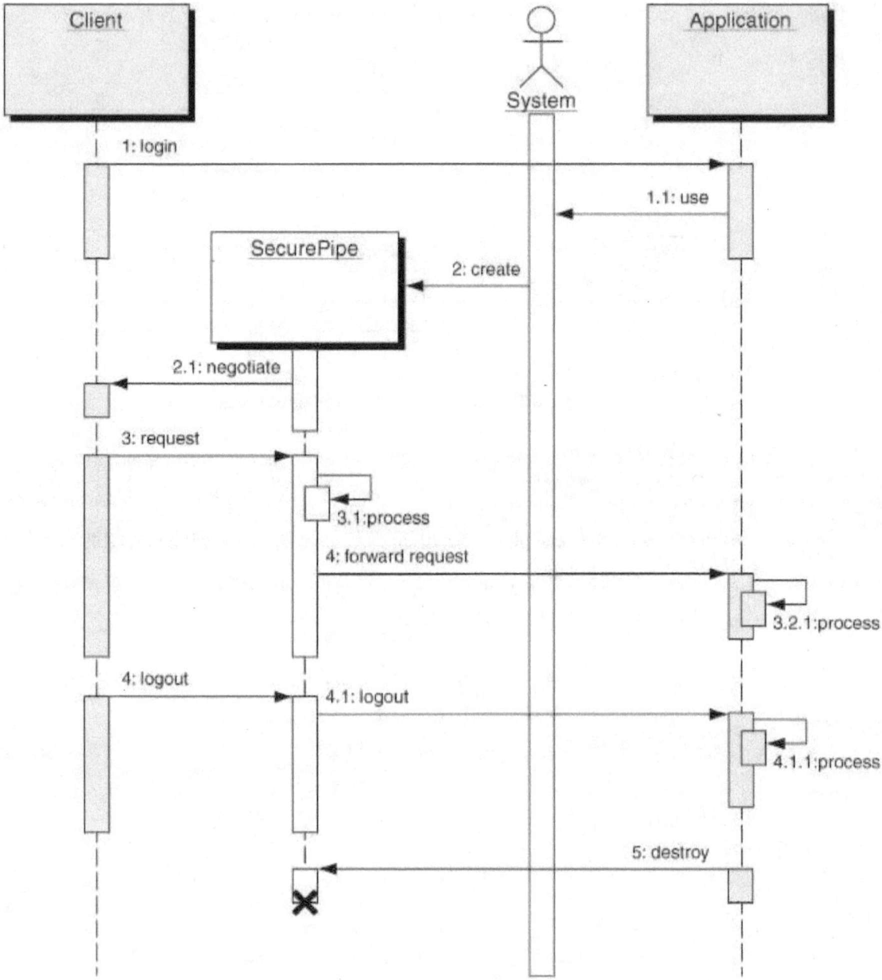


**Figure 3: Sequence Diagram of the Secure Pipe Pattern [42]**

In above figure, to start a communication over the secure communication channel, a client will first need to connect itself to the application.

I will be explaining the step-by-step process of the sequence of secure pipe pattern. It consists of eight steps which are as follows:

a. First, the client sent a login request to the Application.
b. When the application receives the request from the client, it uses the system to create a secure pipe for the communication.
c. Secure pipe then negotiates different security parameters in regard to the connection with the client.
d. Once the parameter had been negotiated, clients sent a request to the application
e. Secure Pipe receives the request and processes it and then creates a secure message by encrypting the data. After the secure message had been created it then send the data to the corresponding Secure Pipe components on the application.
f. Secure Pipe on the Application end receives the encrypted message and decrypts it and then forward the actual request to the application.
g. Once the request had been successfully processed, client sent a logout request.
h. When the application receives the client request for logout it destroys the secure pipe.

The Secure Pipe patterns consist of two components a] client-side components and b] server-side components [43]. Both this components work together to establish secure communication channel. Typically, these components would be SSL or TLS libraries that the Client`s Web browser and the application use for secure communication.

Therefore, the problem of eavesdropping had been successfully resolved by the implementation of secure pipe pattern in web-application as it provide secure communication channel between the client and web-application. Secure pipe guarantees that only the legitimate receiver will receive the message and will able to retrieve the message.

Related pattern for Secure Pipe is Message interceptor Gateway. Message Interceptor Gateway works on gateway level.

As you know gateway mean a single point access point from where all the inbound and outbound traffic comes and goes out from the network. As the web services is always vulnerable to content based attack from an authorized parties and also the traditional firewall and intrusion detection system gives security limited to the IP address ,TCP ports, protocols and packet attack, they does not gives the security to application level.

Therefore the security entry point should be placed for verifying all inbound request and outbound responses. Along with that a proper logging and monitoring mechanism should also be placed. Hence as a result all request will be intercepted and would be verify according to the policy and then it will allowed to enter into the network and same will be done to the outbound response.

The motivation in regard to single access point is that we need to make sure that direct access to application will be difficult. Any access will have to pass through the policy check before it gets access to the application. Also the request or response will be verified for integrity and confidentiality during the transmission so that the eavesdropping and tampering can be detected.

The message interceptor gateway pattern serves as the proxy for the application because it encapsulates access to all access point of the application and provides a centralized access point. It also acts as a decision maker who basically decides whether the particular access request should be passed or not based on the policy enforced. It also secure the inbound and outbound traffic by the securing the communication between the client and the server.

I will be explaining the work of message interceptor gateway with the aid of a diagram which is as follows:

**Figure 4 Message Interceptor Gateway Pattern**

In the above figure,

a. Client – This is a client of message interceptor gateway which is basically web services endpoints that initiates traffic as well also respond to the service requested. So based on the figure the client initiated a request message.
b. The request is intercepted by the Message interceptor gateway and then it processes the request according to the security policy enforced. Based on the policy it may allow or deny further processing of the request.
c. If the request successfully passes the first security verification then it is further processed to check the transport –layer security such as integrity and confidentiality of the request by identifying the uniqueness of the request through timestamp, correlation and ordering etc.
d. After the above process had been successful, the request will then pass to the Message Inspector who checks the authorization and authentication of the request based on the authorization and authentication policy. This information about the authentication and authorization of an identity accessing the services are store into a user repository represented by Identity provider.

e. Lastly after the request will be totally process it will be pass on to the Service Endpoint and the task will be accomplished as requested by the client. Once the task will be completed the response will be generated and will be handed over to the message interceptor gateway in order to pass over the response in a secure way to the client informing him that the request had been successfully processed.

Therefore this is how the message interceptor gateway patterns works to process the request and response of the web-application in a more secure way. The mechanism of checking the integrity and confidentiality which is deployed by the message gateway pattern basically address the problem of eavesdropping and tampering. [44]

### 6.2.2 Mitigating poor authentication exploit with Secure Proxy & its Related Pattern

Poor authentication makes possible for a malicious user to access resources for which they are not authorized to access. Therefore a mechanism should be place in web-application which basically takes care of the authentication and authorization of the request made.

To address this problem into the web-application, secure service proxy pattern had been introduced. Secure proxy pattern provides the services of authentication and authorization of the client or processes that indented to access the services of the web-application.

Secure service proxy intercept all the requests by the clients and then verify the request with the enforced security policy and once the verification is done, it forward the request to the destination services. Later the response by the destination services is formatted according to the specified requirement of the client by the secure service proxy and then it is transmitted to the client. Secure service proxy can be implemented to provide the service of authentication, authorization and other security related services because it can easily be integrated into existing web-application even if the applications are legacy systems.

One of the significant advantage of the deploying the secure service proxy pattern is that it helps the developer to develop a web-application without much worrying about the protocol details from the implementation point of view because its allow multiple client who used different network protocol to access the same services that's expect one particular protocol.

I will explain secure service proxy pattern with the aid of a diagram which are as follows:

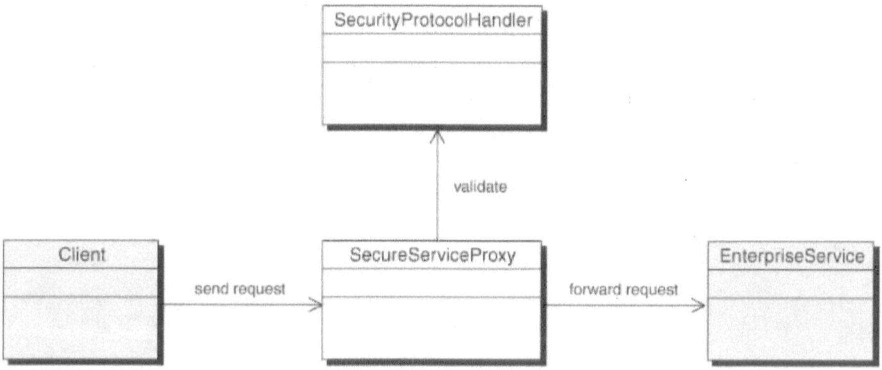


**Figure 5 Secure Service Proxy Pattern Diagram**

In the Figure 1.5 a client sent a request from a web browser to the application which in this diagram is termed as "Enterprise Service". Secure Service Proxy intercepted the request done by the client and sent it to Security protocol handler to validate the request made by the client. Once the request validation is successful then the request is forwarded by the Secure Service Proxy to the application for processing.

Now I will be explaining the sequence of secure proxy pattern which take places on the above specified diagram via the aid of a second diagram which is as follows:

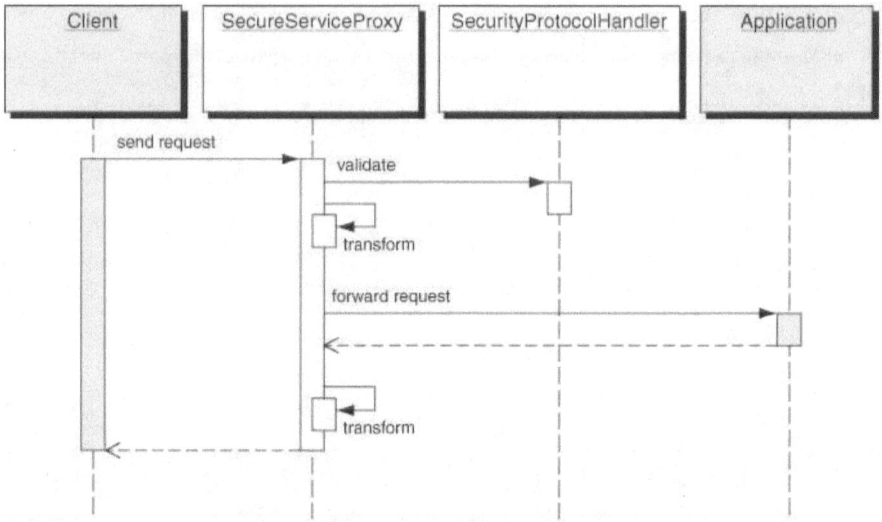


**Figure 6 the sequence diagram of secure proxy pattern**

The sequences are as follows:

a. Client sent request to the Application.[Enterprise Service]
b. Secure Service Proxy intercepted the request made by the client.
c. Secure Service Proxy had used the security protocol handler to verify the request.
d. Once the request is verified, secure service proxy transform the request to the protocol supported by the application.
e. After the transformation of the request protocol is done, it is then forwarded to the application.
f. Once the application processes the request it generates a response which is again transform by the secure service proxy to the appropriate protocol supported by the client.
g. After the transformation, the response is forwarded to the client.

Therefore with the implementation of Secure Service Proxy, the problem of poor authentication is resolved as the request made by the client had been check or validated through the authentication and authorization mechanism of the secure service proxy.[45]

The Related pattern for secure service proxy is message interceptor gateway which I have already discussed above.

### 6.2.3 Mitigating Log Tampering with Secure Logger & its Related Pattern

System log is one the most important mechanism of the system because it contains information which is of great importance to people who basically administrate or troubleshoot the system.

On the other hand it also contains information which is of great importance to an attacker as the attacker can use that information to devise new matrix for attacking the system. Also an attacker can mislead the audit trail by modifying the log data during the attack and can hide their attack.

The implementation of secure logger pattern prevents the system log from being accessed by an attacker and also protects the system log being edited by attacker in order to hide his attack.

I will be explaining the working of the secure logger pattern through the aid of a diagram which is as follows:

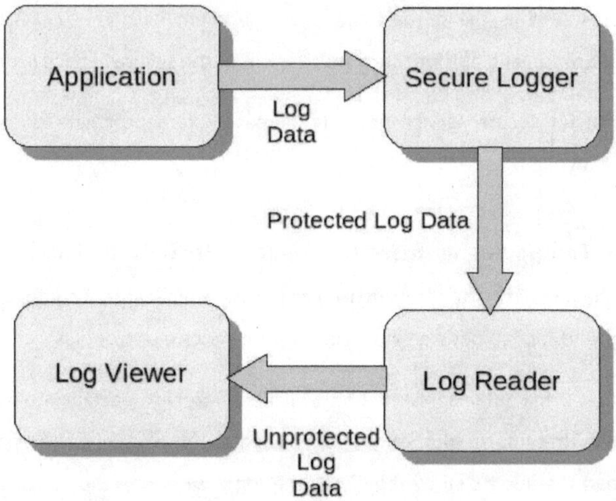


**Figure 7 Secure Logger Pattern Structure**

As shown in the figure 1.7 applications generate the log data which should be stored securely and to accomplish this task secure logger had been used.

Secure logger takes the responsibilities of the storing the log data in such way that it will infeasible or might be impossible for an unauthorized users to access the system log.

Secure logger also engaged the log reader which will be used for reading the log of the system which is protected by the secure logger. Anyone who wants to read the logging data through a standard reader will not be able to read the log of the system as it does not work on the log protected by secure logger.

This protected log can be read by the log viewer only if the user is authorized to read the log.

Therefore even if an attacker had managed to enter the system he will not be able to access the log of the system protected by the secure logger pattern. Hence the attacker will not be able to use the log information to plan his new matrix of attack and also the modification of the logging data will be impossible for an attacker to achieve. [46]

The related pattern for secure logger pattern is secure pipe which I have already explained on the earlier section of this chapter but it actually does not gives the same functionality as compared to secure logger pattern rather its play a very vital role in making the log secure . Therefore I will explain how secure logger pattern works with secure pipe with the aid of a diagram which are as follows:

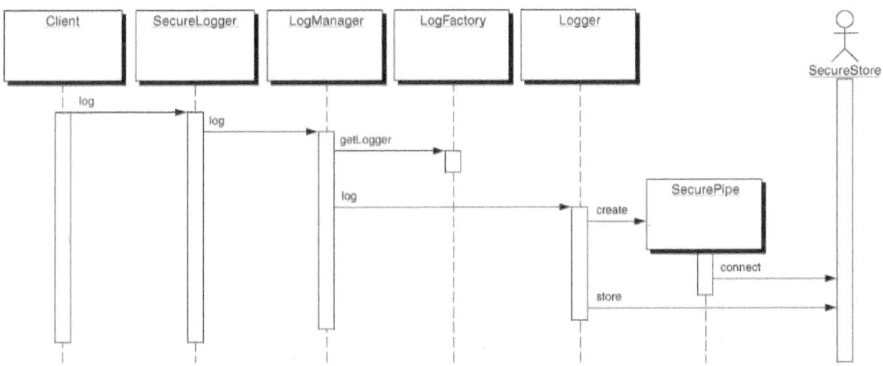


**Figure 8 Secure logger pattern using secure pipe pattern diagram**

As you know that secure logger pattern is responsible for logging the system log securely. Sometime in its strategies of logging the data it basically uses secure pipe. Basically secure logger uses the secure communication to log the data on to the secure log store.

As shown in the figure above once the log is totally generated and passes on to the logger to log the data into secure log Store then logger uses the secure pipe to create a secure communication channel between the logger and the secure log store. Once the secure communication channel had been established then the logger starts storing the data securely to the secure log store. This helps the logger in preventing the log from being modified, deleted or unauthorized access to log entries during transmission.

### 6.2.4 Mitigating SQL Injection, Cross- Site Scripting and HTTP Response Splitting with Intercepting Validator and its Related Pattern

All this attack is one of the most significant attacks which are happening in the web environment around the world. Also there is increase in this kind of attack because the business was shifted from a normal environment to the web environment in the entire sector such as private, public or government organization.

All this attack happens because of the absence of input validation in web-applications. Therefore we need a mechanism which can scan and validate the data passed in by the client. This kind of attack can only be prohibited if the application has a mechanism which can intercept the input and scrub the data before it can be used by the application.

The solutions to above problem is the implementation of intercepting validator pattern which will validate and clean the data before it can be used by the application with the help of dynamically loadable validation logic.

I would be explaining the work of intercepting validator pattern with the help of a diagram which is as follows:

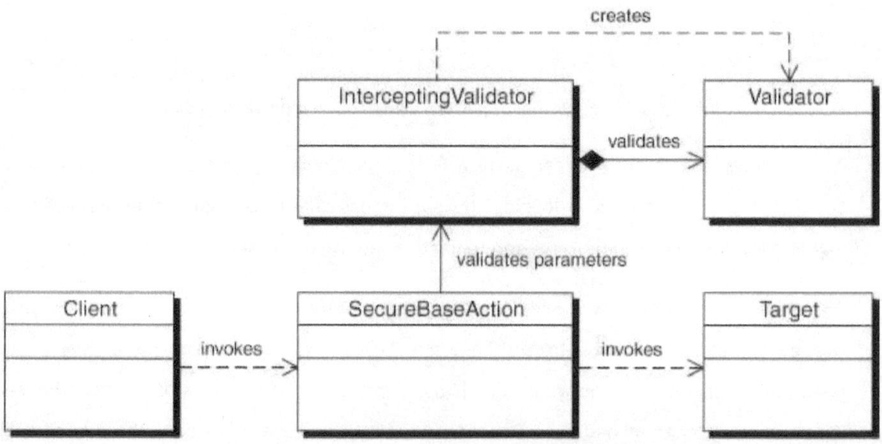


**Figure 9 Intercepting Validator pattern diagram**

As shown on the figure above, client sent a request to the target resources. The secure base action which is deployed by the client is basically taking care for enforcing the validation of input. This mechanism gives the responsibilities of validating the data to intercepting validator.

The interceptor validator takes the data which are to be validated from the secure base action and forward the data to the Validator for validating.

The Validator is responsible for validating the entire input request. Its takes the input and check the format of the data and also examine the data against the parameter for cross-site scripting and other malformed vulnerabilities which are found in URLs. If the request consists of any SQL statement then it is forwarded to the SQL Validator which will validate the request against the parameter set for SQL statement execution. However the sql validator is not mentioned on this figure but it is mentioned on the diagram below which I am going to discuss.

The step-by-step sequence of the Intercepting Validator pattern is as follows:

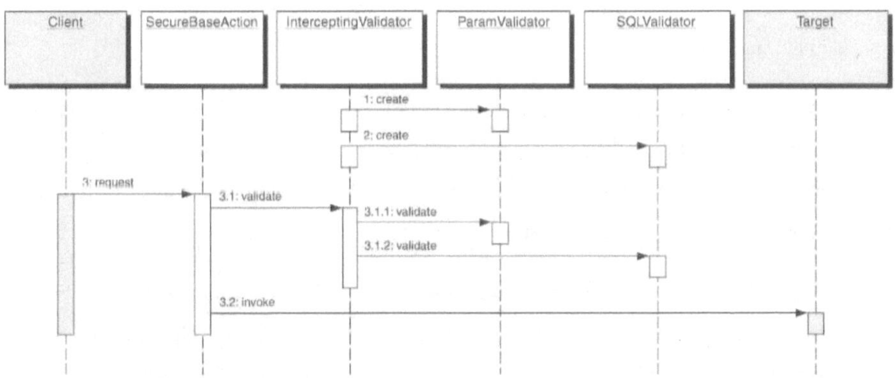


**Figure 10 the sequence diagram of Intercepting Validator Pattern diagram**

As shown on the above figure, the steps are as follows:

a. First the client makes the request to access the resource which in this diagram is stated as target.

b. Secure base actions which basically deploy the intercepting validator takes the request and pass in to the intercepting validator for the validation of data.
c. The intercepting validator contacts the appropriate validator as per the configuration of the target.
d. Intercepting validator invokes a number of different validator and each validator validates and scrubs the data if it is necessary as per the configuration of the target.
e. After the successful validation of data, secure base action forwarded the request to the target for processing.

The concept of deploying different validator for validation is to validate different types of data. For example certain input need to be validated for its size whereas some data are validated against SQL character validation to make sure that the SQL statement cannot be entered into the application.

Therefore with the implementation of Intercepting validator pattern, the above specified attack known as 'SQL Injection', 'Cross- Site Scripting' and 'HTTP Response Splitting' can be addressed as the intercepting validator does the validation of the input which is the primary cause for this kind of attack. [47]

Related Pattern for intercepting validator pattern is intercepting filters. Intercepting filters is one of the powerful tools for eliminating attack such as injection flaws, cross-site scripting etc. The intercepting filters works differently as compare to intercepting validator patter and also it is design pattern not a security pattern.

When the request had been received by the web server for a resource then the web server forwards this request to the intercepting filters. The intercepting filter maintains a list of different kind of filters for the specified resource and activates all filters for validating the request. The request as to go through all the filters and once the request is successfully validated by all the filter, the intercepting filters passes the request to the web-application for processing and generating the response in regard to the request.

In my view both intercepting validator and intercepting filters are the most effective security patterns for giving concrete and robust solution to the above stated problems. However with the shift and advancement in technologies, this kind of attack is becoming more advance in their nature of operation and therefore we should have up-to-date solutions to the future problems. [48]

# Chapter 7: Analysis of Security Patterns

## 7.1 Analysis between main security pattern and related pattern

In this section I will be explaining the benefits and liabilities of implementing the pattern between the main security pattern and related security pattern in detail along with my view and researcher view about the patterns. The style which I will use for addressing this section of my thesis will be summary based. However I will divide the sections into four major sections in discussing the patterns.

### 7.1.1 Secure Pipe Pattern versus Message Intercepting Gateway

Benefits of Secure Pipe Pattern and Message Intercepting Gateway:

I have already explained on my earlier chapters about the working of this pattern in detail with the help of a diagram. However the after effect of the implementation is one the most vital part of any implementation.

There are several strategies which are followed by the industry expert to implement secure pipe pattern such web-based SSL/TLS, Hardware-based, where cryptographic card had been installed to enhance the processing time and lastly with the help of the network hardware which act as the dedicated endpoints for SSL/TLS where as the strategies followed for implementing message interceptor gateway is different. Message interceptor gateway can be applied with the help of network appliances such as firewall etc. However the other way of implementing the message interceptor gateway is through the pluggable agent module. These pluggable agent modules can be configured on the web-server or application server and serves as the infrastructure which manages the information and security policies of the application server.

Secure pipe pattern take cares of the confidentiality and integrity of data during communication by establishing secure channel for communication. Both these services are provided with the help of encryption and digital signature as its uses the SSL/TLS protocol.

Message intercepting gateway also provides transport level security by intercepting the message and verifying the message for confidentiality, integrity and non-repudiation. However its gives some of the extra functionality which secure pipe pattern does not provide. Since it is implemented at gateway level it also safeguard the web-application from DOS attack, brute-force message replay attack, malicious payload attack and man-in-the middle attack. Moreover as it is controlled centrally it can provide management services such as authentication, authorization, audit trails, off-loading etc.

On the other hand secure pipe pattern provides great flexibility in interoperability with the help of the industry infrastructure product and standard protocol such as SSL/TLS, IPSec. Moreover by implementing hardware based cryptographic processing module gives a enhance performance in the overall application level processing. Lastly one of the most vital benefits of the secure pipe pattern is its reduced complexity. Secure pipe pattern basically does the separation of complex cryptographic algorithm from application logic. The procedures of providing secure communication are further pushed to the infrastructure level and the application will only take care of the business logic which makes the application lightweight and highly productive.

Liabilities of Secure Pipe Pattern and Message Intercepting Gateway

Secure pipe pattern is the internal part of web –application architecture and to provide confidentiality and integrity its uses the industry standard known as SSL/TLS. It is totally dependent on this protocol because without this protocol secure pipe pattern implementation will become very complex and management will be bottle neck. Also there is involvement of trusted third party such as certificate authority to deal with public key management and trust model. The vital point out here is that this trusted third parties also come up with lots of issues in their operation and it won't be good idea for the developer to fully rely on the third party for certificate chain management. However it helps the developer to take the benefit of certificate chain to ensure that only authenticate client got access to the web-application. Lastly one of the major drawbacks of implementing secure pipe pattern is the performance, because it requires lots of cryptographic processing its performance is always a question in developer community.

On the other hand message interceptor gateway pattern should have a high availability, the application basically demand 100 percent availability because it is one of the major component in the architecture of web-services as failure in providing such availability will result in financial loss to the organization and may also result in security vulnerabilities. Finally message interceptor gateway should be fault-tolerant to support its critical infrastructure because in an event of failure it can be easily replaced and the working of infrastructure does not jeopardize any processing of the inbound and outbound request or response. Both this situation which are discussed above is very difficult to accomplished from the practical point of view and hope the researcher would able to come up with some solutions to this problem in future.

### 7.1.2 Secure service proxy versus message interceptor gateway

Benefits of Secure Service Proxy and Message Interceptor gateway are-

a. Secure service proxy can act as an application firewall. It`s protects the web application from malicious request. It also performs NAT [network address translation] in order to protect the web-application from the outside world. The most vital benefits of secure service proxy are its capabilities of translating the protocol as per the requirement by the client and web-application. Moreover secure proxy pattern can easily be integrated with the legacy system and takes the responsibilities of authentication and authorization of its request and response. On the other hand message interceptor gateway which works on the gateway level gives different function ability as compared to secure service proxy.
b. Message intercepting gateway provides transport level security by intercepting the message and verifying the message for confidentiality, integrity and non-repudiation. Since it is implemented at gateway level it also safeguard the web-application from DOS attack, brute-force message replay attack, malicious payload attack and man-in-the middle attack. Moreover as it is controlled centrally it can provide management services such as authentication, authorization, audit trails, off-loading etc

Liabilities of Secure Proxy Pattern and Message intercepting gateway are-

a. As per the literature there are no major liabilities of the secure proxy pattern. However as the secure proxy pattern cater to large number of client with the same interface. Therefore the specification of such an interface should be properly communicated among the client for better and smooth operation of the secure proxy pattern.
b. On the other hand message intercepting gateway pattern should have a high availability, the application basically demand 100 percent availability because it is one of the major component in the architecture of web-services as failure in providing such availability will result in financial loss to the organization and may also result in security vulnerabilities. Finally message interceptor gateway should be fault-tolerant to support its critical infrastructure because in an event of failure it can be easily replaced and the working of infrastructure does not jeopardize any processing of the inbound and outbound request or response. Both this situation which are discussed above is very difficult to accomplished from the practical point of view and hope the researcher would able to come up with some solutions to this problem in future.

### 7.1.3 Secure logger pattern versus secure pipe pattern

Secure logger pattern which are used to securely store system log into secure log store. One of the most important benefits of secure logger pattern is its centralized logging control which enables the secure logger to manage logging mechanism centrally which further enhance its reusability and maintainability.

The key to any attack is to hide the attack from audit trail but with the implementation of secure logger, a developer can protect the log from being modified by an attacker ensuring that any attack to the system will be detected during the log file forensics. Moreover as you know security is evolving process, therefore the code should be adaptable or extensible in order to makes changes by the developer, secure logger pattern play an important role by hiding the detail of implementation behind a generic interface which basically expand the lifespan of the code and this code can be tested to make it a bug free code. Lastly secure logger perform all the security processing before saving the logging data to secure log store which allows the secure logger to manage each function independently without risking the overall security impact.

On the other hand secure pipe play a vital role in making the secure logger more secure which will be discussed into the liabilities section of secure logger pattern.

Liabilities of Secure Logger Pattern:

As you know that secure logger pattern is responsible for logging the system log securely which mean the secure logger should encrypt the data before it stores the date to the secure log or rather used secure communication channel to transmit the data securely to secure log store. Either way, management of key which is one of the major issues must be addressed because if the key is not managed properly then the entire secure logger implementation makes no sense. Moreover the confidentiality of the log data should be provided by the secure logger when communicating with secure log store. If the secure logger fails to provide the secure channel for communication then it may be possible that an attacker can intercept the traffic and get some information about the system. Therefore to address this issue secure logger pattern employ the secure pipe pattern who in turn established a secure communication channel for the secure logger so that it can log the system log to the secure log store securely.

### 7.1.4 Intercepting Validator versus Intercepting Filters

Benefits of Intercepting Validator and Intercepting Filters

As you know Intercepting Validator helps in validating the request against malicious code and data injection attack, it's one of the most vital functions is its ability to run data validation centrally. By doing the validation centrally its makes sure that the code is more maintained and reusable. Intercepting validator makes sure that input validation which is one of the main causes of web-application vulnerabilities should be addressed into more systematic and standardized way. Also its implementation practice consists of separating the request validation from presentation logic which basically result in better software and clean coding. Moreover its flexibility in adding new validator module to the existing is out of the question, developer can add new validator module dynamically if the new attack had been captured and the system needs not to be upgraded. [49]

On the other hand intercepting filter is basically a component which is design to intercept inbound request and outbound responses. It activates the list of filter in order to check input validation of the request and response. These filters are different from each other and the data had to be passed from filter to another for complete validation. This mechanism of intercepting filter makes its very popular for address the issues such injection attack, cross-site scripting attack etc. However there is not much literature about the intercepting filter in security pattern community because this filter is the part of design pattern not security pattern.

Liabilities of Intercepting Validator and intercepting filter pattern

The one and the only liabilities of the intercepting validator is the processing overhead. Intercepting validator have to verify each and every request and response for web-application because if it fails in doing such validation then it will result in several attack such SQL injection, cross-site scripting etc .Therefore processing each request and response for the validation effects the overall performance of the intercepting validator.

On the other hand I have not found much literature on the liabilities part of the intercepting filter pattern because it is part of design pattern.

## 7.2 Views

The importance of web-application security had been derived from the evidence that most of the attack on web-application happens due to poorly written code and improper design. This is where security pattern play vital role as it gives some level of security to the application during the design phase.

So far I am discussing different aspect of security pattern which consists of security pattern implementation, benefits and liabilities of pattern and how this pattern is solving the problem of the web-application but the actual motive of describing these aspects of security pattern is to support my view about how the use of this security pattern in web-application is adding value to the overall security infrastructure of the web-application.

To support my view I will be discussing one of the white papers where the researcher proved that security pattern play very vital role in building secure infrastructure of web-application.

The academia named Spyros T. Halkidis, Alexander Chatzigeorgiou and George Stephanides from the department of applied informatics, University of Macedonia had done a Quantitative Evaluation of System with Security Pattern using a fuzzy approach to prove the concept.[50]

In their paper they tried to demonstrate the knowledge by building two separate systems for testing the web-application where one does not include security pattern and the other includes security pattern from design phase itself. Also to perform their analysis they had deployed the AppScan Web Application Penetration testing tools to experiment to what extent the application can sustain the attack as compared between the two systems. In their analysis they had used J2EE environment for both the application into the system as J2EE is widely used in e-commerce platform by business community and for application server they had used JBoss 4.0.3 and MySQL 5.0 for the database.

Later they had purposely left security holes on the first application which the attacker can exploit such as sources of SQL injection, several other sources of Cross –site Scripting and Http Response Splitting sources. Furthermore to make the analysis more interesting they have not configured SSL connection for the first application which makes possible for an attacker to gain critical information such as login credentials though eavesdropping.

On the other hand in the second application, all the security loopholes are not removed but security pattern had been deployed for protecting the system from the attacks. The pattern which are included into the application are Secure proxy pattern, login tunnel pattern, secure pipe pattern, secure logger pattern, secure log store strategy, intercepting validator pattern and container managed security pattern.

Lastly the analysis of both the system had been started and with the help of AppScan penetration testing tool it had been found by them that all the major security flaws in the first application had been identified such as SQL injection, cross-site scripting etc. AppScan also found buffer overflow vulnerabilities and unencrypted request flaws in the first application which does not use SSL. Additionally AppScan also found SSL parameters flaws in the second application but it does not possess high risk to the second application

However they found out that flaw in security of second application are fewer as compare to the first application. After they have carefully analyzed they have concluded that the proper use of security pattern in second application actually prevent the application from the above specified attacks. They have also found out that intercepting validator pattern play a vital role in validating all kind of inputs which includes sessions variables as well due to which attack such as SQL injection, cross-site scripting and HTTP response splitting cannot able to take place.

Secondly the inclusion of secure proxy pattern and login tunnel pattern which they have deployed has two level of authentication mechanism in the application which had prevented the application from spoofing, Elevation of privileges and disclosure of information. Thirdly with the help of secure pipe pattern they found out that the application is able to create secure communication channel which further defeats eavesdropping attack when the application communicates with the client [web browser].

Lastly they have found out that secure logger pattern helps the application in logging the log data securely to the secure log store thus protecting the log date from being tampered or modified.

Finally the researcher had concluded from their analysis that the system which includes security pattern during their design phase is highly secure and robust to attack then the system which does not employ security patterns in their design.

Therefore, I would conclude that security pattern should be given at most priority during the design and development phase of any software and web-application so that we can have secure infrastructure from the base and thus succeed in providing security to our critical information as a whole.

## Conclusion

While exploring how security can be incorporated by using security patterns in web-application, I have come across many important points which I would like to have answer in the near future.

Before, I say something about the point I would like to tell you that in my entire paper I have seen that security patterns really plays a very vital role in the development of secure application. In fact company like Microsoft and Sun Microsystem had their own department of patterns and practices. Additionally, JAVA which is widely used in the development of the web-application have separate packages known as Java.Security which heavily follows the pattern languages in their implementation and the most important thing in my entire thesis is basically a expansion of JAVA Security Framework which follows security pattern such as Web-Tier Security Pattern and Web –Services Security Patterns.

As I have discussed some of the major security patterns in my thesis and also enlighten you about how this patterns work and what are their benefits and liabilities I would like to say some important point which I feel that this pattern had not answered in addressing the security problems.

First of all, if you take secure pipe pattern then you can see that it only provide secure communication channel by establishing the secure connection between client and server. However, what if the server with whom the client is communicating is been controlled by an attacker? The client thinks it is communicating with a genuine server. Thus the solution to this problem is a trusted third party. But secure pipe pattern is integral part of web-application so there should be some mechanism internally which ensures that the client is communicating to the genuine server.

Secondly, Message interceptor gateway pattern is the one which provide more robust security to the web-application as compared to secure pipe pattern but since its checks all the response and request of the web-application, performance is one of the major questions. Additionally, It also provide other services such as integrity and confidentiality to the web-application, which again is not feasible from the security point of view as one mechanism should not provide all functionality of security because if this mechanism is compromised then the entire security will collapse.

Thirdly, secure proxy pattern provides solutions where each request are validated through the authentication and authorization mechanism before it get access to resource of web-application. However what I would like to say about the above pattern is that if the malicious user can get hold of the password of the legitimate user and masquerade, then the issues is still unresolved. Hence a proper training and awareness program should be built to make the user aware about the security aspect of the system. Moreover, it does not deploy any dual authentication mechanism so that a second line defence can be built if the first line of defence is broken. Thus, I think though it gives some kind of assurance in regard to authentication and authorization of the user it still lack a full proof solutions of the problems and therefore I will highly recommend that there should be something more robust security pattern could be discovered to address the above stated issues

Fourthly, Secure logger pattern which basically log the system log securely so that it cannot be modified or tampered by an attacker. However, I think that the problem remains the same, suppose if an attacker get hold of a login credential of a legitimate user then he can securely login with credential and make changes to the audit log and thus hide his attack.

I think there should be some kind of dual authentication mechanism which could be placed which basically serves the purpose of authenticating the user before he/she can access the log. I think secure logger pattern just gives the basic security in securing log and we need something more robust to address the issue as a whole.

These are some of the point which I think that it would be considered in the research world and all this point could be considered during the designing of security patterns in near future. Rest I can say that security pattern had at least given us some sense of security as whole and made the web-application secure in this world of public communication and hope it will provide more robust solutions in the future

However, the researcher community have different view about the security patterns. They believe that for the secure development of software , a secure design should emerged and this secure design is nothing but "Security Pattern" which can address security issues at different levels of abstraction. Presently, Dr. Eduardo Fernandez is doing extensive research in security patterns and had published many papers on this subject. Some of his very good work is presented in http://www.computer.org/portal/web/tdsc/ .

Future Work

The researcher is presently working in developing the tools which follows the security pattern and which will help the developer to develop code with less security flaws. They are also coming up with the centralized repository for security patterns where all security patterns will be kept for future reference and development. This repository will be used by the big software organization in their process for developing secure software.

## References


[1] Boxes and Arrows, What is a Web Application?
http://www.boxesandarrows.com/view/what_is_a_web_application_, August Issue, 2011

[2]. Boxes and Arrows, What is a Web Application?
http://www.boxesandarrows.com/view/what_is_a_web_application_, August Issue, 2011

[3]. The J2ee 1.4 Tutorial, Getting Started with Web Application, http://download .oracle .com /javaee/1.4/tutorial/doc/WebApp.html, August, 2011

[4]. About.com Web Trends, Web Application, What is a Web Application?
http://webtrends.about.com/od/webapplications/a/web_application.htm , August,2011

[5]. Acunetix Web Application Security, Web-Applications: What are they? What of them?
http://www.acunetix.com/websitesecurity/web-applications.htm, August, 2011

[6]. "Trending From Keyword Gimmicks Towards Customer Service Based ...."
http://juliatew.com/?p=1 23 Aug. 2011

[7]. "Slide 1." 03 Jun. 2009, http://www.isaca-oregon.org/docs/SPI_WORKSHOP_PRESO_Worm_Hack2.ppt 23 Aug. 2011.

[8]. Out- Law.com , FBI computer Crime and Security Survey Results, http://www.out-law.com/page-2508 , August, 2011

[9]. SearchFinancialSecurity.com, Eavesdropping,
http://searchfinancialsecurity.techtarget.com/definition/eavesdropping, August, 2011

[10]. Haidong Xia and Jos´e Carlos Brustoloni, Hardening Web Browsers against Man-in-the-Middle and Eavesdropping Attacks,http://www2005.org/cdrom/docs/p489.pdf ,August 2011

[11]. Tcpdump , http://www.tcpdump.org/

[12]. Ethereal , http://www.ethereal.com/

[13]. Microsoft Patterns & Practices, Chapter 2 Threats and Countermeasures,
http://msdn.microsoft.com/en-us/library/ff648641.aspx#c02618429_006, January,2006

[14]. Webopedia, System Log, http://www.webopedia.com/TERM/S/system_log.html , August, 2011

[15]. CAPEC, CAPEC-93: Log Injection,Tampering,Forging, http://capec.mitre.org/data/definitions/93.htmlAugust,2011

[16]. Scribd Explore, OWASP TOP 10 for JAVA EE, http://www.scribd.com/doc/54417096/6/A2-%E2%80%93-INJECTION-FLAWS , August, 2011

[17]. Amit Klein, Cross Site Scripting Explained, http://crypto.stanford.edu/cs155/papers/CSS.pdf, June, 2002

[18]. WatchFire, Amit Klein, DIVIDE AND CONQUER, http://doc.hackbbs.org/Reseaux/HTTP%20Response%20Splitting.pdf, August, 2011

[19]. Core Security Patterns Weblog, Http response splitting, How to prevent them J2ee/Web-Application? http://www.coresecuritypatterns.com/blogs/?p=128 , August, 2011

[20]. Victor Lombardi, Pattern Languages for Interaction Design, http://www.noisebetweenstations.com/personal/essays/intro_to_pattern_languages.pdf , August, 2011.

[21]. Alexander Christopher, the Timeless Way of Building, Oxford University Press, 1979.

[22]. Design Pattern: Elements of Reusable Object- Oriented Software, Addison-Wesley, 1995

[23]. Victor Lombardi, Pattern Languages for Interaction Design, http://www.noisebetweenstations.com/personal/essays/intro_to_pattern_languages.pdf , August, 2011.

[24]. William H. Mitchell, An Introduction to Design Patterns, http://www.mitchellsoftwareengineering.com/IntroToDesignPatterns.pdf August, 2011.

[25]. Design Pattern: Elements of Reusable Object- Oriented Software, Addison-Wesley, 1995

[26]. Pattern: Cult to Culture? In proceeding of OOPSLA `95, Austin, Texas, USA, 1995

[27]. D Janaki Ram, K N Anantha Raman, A Pattern Oriented Technique for Software Design, http://dos.iitm.ac.in/LabPapers/ACMsenPOT.pdf , July, 1997.

[28]. William H. Mitchell, An Introduction to Design Patterns, http://www.mitchellsoftwareengineering.com/IntroToDesignPatterns.pdf August, 2011.

[29]. Webopedia, Pattern, http://www.webopedia.com/TERM/P/pattern.html,August, 2011

[30]. Markus Schumacher and Utz Roedig. Security engineering with patterns. In 8th Conference on Pattern Languages of Programs, July 2001.

[31]. Science Direct, Automated verification of security pattern compositions, http://www.sciencedirect.com/science/article/pii/S0950584909001724 ,October, 2009.

[32]. Richard Lewis, What is Security Pattern, http://secureapps.blogspot.com/2006/08/what-is-security-pattern.html ,August, 2006.

[33]. Markus Schumacher, Foundation of Security Pattern, http://www.springerlink.com/content/n6n0jh9vyw5qdbvu/fulltext.pdf, August, 2011

[34]. DARRELL M. KIENZLE, Final Technical Report:Security Patterns for Web Application Development, http://www.scrypt.net/~celer/securitypatterns/final%20report.pdf May,2002

[35]. Eduardo B. Fernandez, Nobukazu Yoshioka, Hironori Washizaki, Jan Jurjens,

Michael VanHilst, and Guenther Pernul, Using security patterns to develop secure systems, http://www-jj.cs.tu-dortmund.de/jj/publications/papers/SecPattsOct30-09a.pdf August, 2011

[36]. Darrell M. Kienzle, Matthew C. Elder, David S. Tyree, Introduction Security Patterns Template and Tutorial,http://citeseerx.ist.psu.edu/viewdoc/summary?doi=10.1.1.131.2464 ,August 2011

[37]. Chris Steel, Ramesh Nagappan, Core Security Patterns, http://www.coresecuritypatterns.com/patterns.htm , August, 2011.

[38]. Econpapers, Security Design Patterns , http://econpapers.repec.org/article/tmujournl/v_3a9_3ay_3a2010_3ai_3a2_3ap_3a31-36.htm, August, 2011

[39]. Science Direct, Automated verification of security pattern compositions, http://www.sciencedirect.com/science/article/pii/S0950584909001724 ,October, 2009.

[40]."Core Security Patterns Best Practices and Design strategies" 27 Aug. 2010, http://www.coresecuritypatterns.com/patterns.htm 23 Aug. 2011

[41]."Implementing Validation Rules using Aspects Java.net, http://www.java.net/pub/a/today/2005/11/08/implementing-validation-ruLes-with-aspects.html, August. 2011

[42]. "Free e books Core Security Patterns. Best Practices and ...." http:// flylib.com/books/en/3.211.1.127/1/ 23 Aug. 2011

[43]. "Free e books Core Security Patterns. Best Practices and ...." http:// flylib.com/books/en/3.211.1.127/1/ 23 Aug. 2011

[44]. Core Security Patterns Best Practices and Strategies for J2EE Web Services and Identity Management, Prentice Hall, October, 2005 chapter 9 page 39 – 43, and chapter 11 page 5 – 13

[45]. Core Security Patterns Best Practices and Strategies for J2EE Web Services and Identity Management, Prentice Hall, October, 2005 chapter 9 page 46 – 52

[46]. Software Engineering Institute, Security Design Patterns, www.cert.org/archive/pdf/09tr010.pdf , August, 2011

[47]. Hohpe, Woolf. Enterprise Integration Patterns. Addison-Wesley, 2004

[48]. Intercepting Filters, Brief Descriptions, http://java.sun.com/blueprints/patterns/InterceptingFilter.html August, 2011

[49]. David Winterfeldt and Ted Husted. Struts in Action, "Chapter 12: Validating User Input.http://java.sun.com/developer/Books/javaprogramming/struts/struts_chptr_12.pdf,August, 2011

[50].Spyros T. Halkidis, Er Chatzigeorgiou, George Stephanides, Quantitative Evaluation of System with Security Pattern using a fuzzy approach, August,2011

www.ingramcontent.com/pod-product-compliance
Lightning Source LLC
La Vergne TN
LVHW102228300926
849160LV00005B/71
* 9 7 8 3 9 5 4 8 9 2 6 6 2 *